RELOCATING TO ALBANIA

A COMPREHENSIVE GUIDE
FOR A SEAMLESS TRANSITION

BY

WILLIAM JONES

2023

Relocating to Albania: A Comprehensive Guide for a Seamless Transition by William Jones

This book edition was created and published by Mamba Press

Contents

Preface

Welcome, fellow traveler, to the pages of "Relocating to Albania: A Comprehensive Guide for a Seamless Transition." Whether you're here out of curiosity, planning a move, or have already taken the plunge into the adventure of relocating to Albania, this guide is crafted with you in mind. As you leaf through these words, envision them as signposts along the path to a new chapter in your life, a chapter set against the backdrop of a country that is as diverse and welcoming as its landscapes are stunning.

Moving to a new country is a journey laden with excitement, trepidation, and the promise of countless new experiences. Albania, with its rich history, warm people, and awe-inspiring landscapes, offers a canvas for a life-altering adventure. This guide seeks to be your compass, helping you navigate the uncharted waters of relocation with confidence and ease.

Why Albania, you may ask? Well, why not? This hidden gem in the heart of the Balkans has been quietly evolving, shedding the remnants of its past and emerging as a destination that beckons with open arms. The warmth of its people, the tapestry of its culture, and the allure of its mountains and coastline make Albania a unique and enchanting choice.

As we embark on this literary journey together, it's important to acknowledge that relocation is more than just changing addresses; it's about weaving yourself into the fabric of a new place, embracing its quirks, celebrating its triumphs, and, in turn, allowing it to shape you. Albania, with its blend of tradition and modernity, offers an immersive experience where every encounter, every twist in the cobblestone road, contributes to the tapestry of your personal story.

So, whether you're here to gather information for an impending move or you're simply dreaming of the possibilities that lie beyond your horizon, let these words be your companions. They are not just a collection of information; they are anecdotes, insights, and guidance from those who have ventured before you, from those who have fallen in love with the warmth of Albanian hospitality, and from those who have come to call this land home.

Consider this preface as a warm handshake from a friend who has already navigated the maze of relocation. We understand the exhilaration of new beginnings and the challenges that may lie ahead. As you read, imagine us sitting across from you, sharing stories over a cup of strong Albanian coffee, laughter echoing against the backdrop of ancient mountains.

This guide is designed to be more than a list of do's and don'ts; it's a conversation about life, culture, and the art of embracing the unknown. It's about discovering not only the practicalities of finding a home and opening a bank account but also the intangibles—the unwritten rules, the unspoken gestures, and the rhythms of daily life that will soon become second nature.

As you turn the pages, you'll find a wealth of information to make your transition smoother—from understanding the legalities of your move to embracing the nuances of the Albanian language. You'll uncover the secrets to finding the perfect dwelling, forging connections with locals, and, most importantly, creating a life that resonates with the beat of Albanian hearts.

So, dear reader, whether you're drawn to the medieval charm of Gjirokastër, the vibrant streets of Tirana, or the azure waters of the Albanian Riviera, remember that every journey begins with a single step. Your step, in this case, is the decision to explore the pages ahead.

Albania awaits—a land where the past whispers through ancient ruins, where the present hums with the rhythm of modernity, and where the future holds the promise of a life well-lived. Let's embark on this journey together, with open hearts and a curiosity that knows no bounds. Welcome to a guide that not only informs but also invites you to savor the essence of relocation—to Albania, a place where the ordinary becomes extraordinary, and the unfamiliar becomes home.

Introduction

Dear Explorer,

Embarking on a journey to a new land is a venture into the unknown—a tapestry woven with threads of anticipation, curiosity, and the thrill of discovery. As you delve into the heart of this guide, "Relocating to Albania: A Comprehensive Guide for a Seamless Transition," consider it your compass, guiding you through the intricate terrain of relocation to a country that is as diverse as its landscapes are breathtaking.

Albania, the jewel nestled in the embrace of the Balkans, awaits your arrival with open arms. Whether you've decided to make the move or are still contemplating the idea, this guide is your trusted companion, a roadmap crafted to transform the intricacies of relocation into a harmonious symphony of experiences.

Before we dive into the practicalities of visas, housing, and cultural nuances, let's take a moment to immerse ourselves in the essence of this enchanting country. Albania, with its rich history dating back to Illyrian times, has weathered the storms of change and emerged as a destination that encapsulates the spirit of resilience and renewal.

Imagine wandering through the cobbled streets of Gjirokastër, where every stone whispers tales of centuries gone by. Picture the vibrant bustle of Tirana, where the modern and the traditional coexist in a captivating dance. Envision the azure waters of the Albanian Riviera, where the Adriatic and Ionian Seas embrace the rugged coastline in a tender caress. Albania is not just a country; it's a mosaic of experiences waiting to be unraveled.

As you stand at the threshold of this adventure, it's only natural to be accompanied by a flurry of questions. Why Albania? What awaits me there? How do I navigate the unfamiliar terrain? Rest assured, these are questions we've grappled with ourselves. The decision to relocate is a profound one, laden with considerations both practical and emotional. And it's precisely these considerations that we aim to address in the chapters that follow.

Now, let's address the proverbial elephant in the room—why choose Albania? It's a question that tugs at the fabric of your decision-making process, and rightfully so. Albania is not the first name that comes to mind when people think of relocation. It's not splashed across glossy travel magazines, nor is it a topic of everyday conversation. But therein lies its allure.

Albania is an undiscovered gem, a canvas waiting for the strokes of your story to bring it to life. It's a land where tradition and modernity waltz hand in hand, where the echoes of communism linger in the remnants of bunkers, juxtaposed against the vibrant energy of a nation embracing its newfound freedom. Albania is a paradox—a country that captivates with its simplicity and surprises with its complexity.

The decision to relocate is multifaceted, shaped by a myriad of factors unique to each individual. Perhaps it's the allure of the Albanian Riviera, where pristine beaches and quaint villages beckon with promises of tranquility. Maybe it's the history, the layers of civilizations etched into the landscape, from ancient Illyrian ruins to Ottoman architecture. Or it could be the warmth of the people, whose hospitality transcends language barriers and makes you feel not like a visitor, but a welcomed guest.

As you read through these pages, think of them as letters from a friend who has ventured before you, a friend who understands the exhilaration of new beginnings and the unease of stepping into the unfamiliar. The guide is more than a compendium of facts; it's a collection of stories, insights, and tips shared by those who have fallen in love with the charm of Albania. It's an invitation to explore not just the practicalities of relocation but also the soul of a country—a tapestry woven with the threads of its people, its history, and its untamed landscapes.

In the chapters ahead, we'll navigate the labyrinth of legalities, housing searches, and cultural adaptation. We'll provide insights into the intricacies of everyday life, from savoring the robust flavors of Albanian cuisine to deciphering the rhythm of the language. But before we delve into the specifics, take a moment to savor the excitement that comes with a blank canvas—a canvas that Albania invites you to fill with the vibrant hues of your unique journey.

Relocation is not just about changing your address; it's about embracing a new way of life. It's about forging connections, creating memories, and allowing the spirit of a place to seep into your very being. Albania, with its quirks, challenges, and unspoken charms, is poised to become the backdrop of your next chapter.

So, dear reader, let's embark on this odyssey together—a journey where the unfamiliar becomes familiar, where the challenges become opportunities, and where the ordinary transforms into the extraordinary. Welcome to the introduction of your Albanian adventure. May these words be the compass that guides you through the exciting chapters that lie ahead.

Chapter 1

Discovering Albania

In the heart of the Balkans, where rugged mountains kiss the sky and azure waters gently caress the coastline, lies a country that has long remained a well-kept secret. Welcome to Albania—a land of ancient traditions, captivating history, and a warm embrace that beckons to those seeking the road less traveled.

Close your eyes for a moment and envision a landscape where olive groves stretch as far as the eye can see, where ancient ruins whisper tales of empires past, and where the scent of wildflowers mingles with the sea breeze. This is the canvas upon which Albania paints its story—an epic that unfolds against the backdrop of the Illyrians, the Romans, the Ottomans, and a struggle for freedom that has shaped its resilient spirit.

To truly discover Albania is to embark on a journey through time, where ancient artifacts seamlessly blend with the pulse of modern life. Illyrian tribes once roamed these lands, leaving behind traces etched in stone, while the Byzantines and Romans carved their legacy into the hillsides. The Ottoman Empire, with its domed mosques and cobbled bazaars, added yet another layer to Albania's cultural tapestry.

As you traverse this enigmatic land, you'll encounter the remnants of communism—a period frozen in the bunkers that dot the countryside. These stark reminders stand in contrast to the vibrant energy of a nation that emerged from isolation to embrace the freedoms of the 20th century.

Albania's landscape is a mosaic of diversity. In the north, the Accursed Mountains cradle pristine lakes and traditional villages, offering a haven for hikers and cultural enthusiasts alike. The central plains unfold like a patchwork quilt, with fertile valleys and historic cities such as Shkodra, where the clash of civilizations is palpable in every stone. And then there's the Riviera, where the Adriatic and Ionian Seas playfully meet, gifting travelers with sun-soaked beaches and charming coastal towns.

Tirana, the beating heart of Albania, is a microcosm of the nation's evolution. From the pastel hues of communist-era buildings to the vibrant street art that adorns the city, Tirana embodies the spirit of a country embracing change while honoring its roots. As you stroll through Skanderbeg Square, named after the national hero who defied the Ottoman Empire, you'll feel the pulse of a city that is both a testament to resilience and a celebration of newfound freedom.

Albania's allure is not confined to its physical beauty; it lies in the warmth of its people. Hospitality here is not a mere custom; it's a way of life. Expect to be greeted with smiles that reflect genuine curiosity and a willingness to share the richness of Albanian culture. Whether you find yourself sipping strong coffee in a local kafene, sampling baklava in a bustling bazaar, or partaking in the spirited festivities of a village celebration, the hospitality of the Albanian people will leave an indelible mark on your journey.

Language, they say, is the key to understanding a culture, and in Albania, it's a key that unlocks a treasure trove of connections. Albanian, with its unique linguistic roots, is a testament to the country's distinct identity. Don't be daunted by the unfamiliar sounds and syntax; instead, embrace the opportunity to learn phrases that will not only help you navigate daily life but also open doors to the hearts of locals.

As you immerse yourself in the language, you'll discover that Albania is a country where the past and present engage in a dance. From the ancient amphitheater of Butrint, a UNESCO World Heritage Site, to the vibrant nightlife of trendy Blloku in Tirana, every step you take is a step through time.

Albania's culinary landscape is a feast for the senses—a symphony of flavors that reflect the nation's diverse history. Savor the robust notes of slow-cooked lamb, indulge in the simplicity of fresh seafood along the coast, and relish the sweetness of baklava as you wander through bustling markets. Dining in Albania is not just a culinary experience; it's an invitation to partake in the traditions and stories that accompany each dish.

Now, as you stand on the threshold of your Albanian adventure, know that you're about to embark on a journey of discovery—a journey that transcends the ordinary and invites you to explore the extraordinary. Albania, with its layers of history, its diverse landscapes, and its warmhearted people, is ready to unfold its secrets before you.

In the chapters that follow, we'll delve into the practicalities of relocation, from understanding legal requirements to finding the perfect dwelling. But as you prepare for the transition, keep in mind that discovering Albania is not just about the logistics; it's about allowing the soul of the country to seep into your own. So, pack your curiosity and let's set forth on a voyage through the enchanting landscapes and the welcoming embrace of Albania—a journey where every step is a revelation and every encounter is an invitation to discover the heart of a nation.

Chapter 2
Planning Your Move

Embarking on a journey to a new country is akin to setting sail on uncharted waters—a mix of excitement, anticipation, and a dash of apprehension. Planning your move to Albania is not merely about changing your geographical coordinates; it's a meticulous dance of considerations, from the practicalities of paperwork to the emotional nuances of acclimating to a new culture. As you embark on this chapter, envision it as a compass guiding you through the labyrinth of relocation, helping you navigate the seas of change with confidence.

Understanding Your Why

Before delving into the intricacies of planning your move, take a moment to reflect on the essence of your decision. Why Albania? What beckons you to this land of mystery and warmth? Understanding your motivations will not only shape the logistics of your move but also infuse your journey with purpose. Whether it's the allure of the Albanian Riviera, the rich historical tapestry, or the promise of a different way of life, let your reasons anchor your decisions.

Setting Clear Goals

Now that you've identified your motivations, it's time to set clear goals for your move. What do you hope to achieve? Are you seeking a change of scenery, pursuing career opportunities, or embracing a new chapter in your personal life? By articulating your goals, you create a roadmap that will guide your decisions throughout the planning process. Whether short-term or long-term, your goals will serve as beacons, ensuring that your move aligns with your aspirations.

Navigating the Legal Waters

One of the initial steps in planning your move is understanding the legal requirements. Research the visa and permit options available for your specific situation. Albania, like any other country, has its own set of regulations, and being well-informed will save you from unnecessary hurdles. Consult the official government websites, reach out to embassies, and consider seeking advice from expatriates who have navigated these waters before you. A clear understanding of the legal landscape will set the foundation for a smooth transition.

Creating a Realistic Budget and Timeline

Finances and timeframes are the backbone of any relocation plan. Begin by creating a comprehensive budget that factors in visa fees, travel expenses, accommodation costs, and potential unforeseen circumstances. Be realistic about your financial capabilities, and consider building a buffer for unexpected expenses. Simultaneously, outline a timeline that encompasses key milestones, from visa applications to the actual move. This timeline will serve as a roadmap, ensuring that each step is taken with due diligence and without unnecessary haste.

Researching Your Destination

As you plan your move, take the time to research your destination in-depth. Albania, with its diverse cities and regions, offers a spectrum of choices. Consider factors such as climate, cost of living, job opportunities, and lifestyle when selecting your destination. Each city and region has its unique charm, and aligning your preferences with the local culture will contribute to a more seamless integration.

Networking and Seeking Advice

In the age of connectivity, networking has become an invaluable resource for expatriates. Tap into online forums, social media groups, and expat communities to connect with individuals who have already made the move to Albania. Their insights, experiences, and advice can be priceless in navigating the nuances of the relocation process. From cultural tips to practical advice on housing and local services, the wisdom shared by those who have walked this path before can be a beacon of guidance.

Preparing for Cultural Adjustment

Moving to a new country entails not only a change of location but also a shift in cultural dynamics. Prepare yourself for cultural adjustment by familiarizing yourself with Albanian customs, traditions, and social norms. Language, as a conduit of culture, plays a pivotal role in this process. While not mandatory, learning basic Albanian phrases will not only enhance your ability to communicate but also demonstrate your commitment to embracing the local way of life.

Considering Healthcare Options

Healthcare is a crucial aspect of any relocation plan. Research the healthcare system in Albania, including available services, insurance options, and the quality of medical facilities. Ensure that you have access to essential healthcare services and that you understand the procedures for emergencies. Familiarize yourself with local pharmacies, hospitals, and medical professionals, creating a safety net for your well-being.

Preparing Your Finances

As you navigate the financial aspects of your move, take the time to prepare your finances for the transition. Notify your bank about your move and inquire about international banking options. Familiarize yourself with the local currency and banking practices in Albania. Establishing a financial plan that includes currency exchange considerations, budget management, and potential tax implications will contribute to a seamless financial transition.

Packing and Decluttering

The physical act of moving involves packing up your life and belongings. Begin the process by decluttering your possessions, evaluating what to keep, sell, donate, or discard. Consider the climate in Albania when deciding what to pack, and prioritize essential items. Remember that your new home is an opportunity for a fresh start, and the act of decluttering can be both liberating and symbolic of embracing change.

Building a Support System

Relocating to a new country can be both exhilarating and challenging. Building a support system is essential for a smoother transition. Reach out to friends, family, or acquaintances who have experience living abroad. Establish connections within the local community and expatri-

ate circles. Having a support system in place, even if it's just a network
of fellow expatriates, provides a sense of camaraderie and understanding
during the initial stages of your journey.

In the intricate dance of planning your move to Albania, each step
is a brushstroke on the canvas of your new life. By understanding your
motivations, setting clear goals, navigating the legal landscape, and embracing the cultural intricacies, you lay the foundation for a successful
transition. As you navigate the seas of change, remember that the journey
is not just about reaching a destination—it's about savoring the process,
immersing yourself in the culture, and allowing the adventure of relocation to shape the next chapter of your life. So, plan deliberately, embrace
the unknown, and prepare for the enchanting journey that lies ahead.

Chapter 3
Choosing Your Destination

Selecting the destination for your new adventure in Albania is akin to choosing the color palette for a painting—you want it to resonate with your preferences, complement your lifestyle, and, most importantly, inspire you every day. In this chapter, let's embark on a journey through the diverse cities and regions of Albania, each offering its own unique charm and character. Whether you're drawn to the medieval allure of Gjirokastër, the vibrant energy of Tirana, or the coastal serenity of the Albanian Riviera, finding your perfect destination is the first step toward creating a life that aligns with your dreams.

Tirana: The Beating Heart of Albania

Begin your exploration with the capital city, Tirana—a vibrant metropolis that stands as a testament to Albania's journey through time. Tirana is a city where the past and present converge in a captivating dance, where communist-era buildings wear pastel hues, and where the skyline is adorned with modern architecture. Skanderbeg Square, named after the national hero who resisted the Ottoman Empire, serves as the central hub, pulsating with life.

In Tirana, you'll find a kaleidoscope of experiences. Dive into the energy of Blloku, once a restricted area during the communist era and now a trendy district teeming with boutiques, cafes, and a lively nightlife. The Pyramid, a remnant of the communist regime, stands as both a historical relic and a testament to the city's resilience.

As the political, cultural, and economic epicenter of Albania, Tirana offers a myriad of job opportunities, educational institutions, and a dynamic expatriate community. The city's diverse culinary scene, from traditional Albanian fare to international cuisine, reflects the openness of Tirana to different cultures.

Shkodra: Where History Meets Tradition

Nestled on the shores of Lake Shkodra, the city of Shkodra is a haven for those seeking a blend of history and natural beauty. Surrounded by mountains and steeped in a rich historical legacy, Shkodra has earned its place as one of Albania's cultural gems.

Take a stroll through the cobbled streets of the Old Town, where Ottoman architecture coexists with medieval influences. Shkodra is a city where the clash of civilizations is palpable, offering a fascinating glimpse into Albania's complex history.

Lake Shkodra, one of the largest in the Balkans, provides a picturesque backdrop for outdoor enthusiasts. The city's proximity to the Albanian Alps makes it an ideal base for hiking and exploring the pristine landscapes of northern Albania.

Gjirokastër: The City of a Thousand Steps

For those captivated by medieval charm and a sense of time standing still, Gjirokastër is a living museum. Perched on a hillside, this UNESCO World Heritage Site exudes a sense of timelessness, with its stone houses, narrow alleys, and a fortress that has witnessed centuries of history.

Known as the "City of a Thousand Steps," Gjirokastër invites you to wander through its cobblestone streets and explore its well-preserved Ottoman architecture. The Gjirokastër Castle, with its commanding views of the city and surrounding mountains, transports you back in time.

In Gjirokastër, life unfolds at a slower pace, allowing you to savor the simple pleasures of daily living. The city's cultural heritage is reflected in its museums, art galleries, and the birthplace of renowned author Ismail Kadare.

Vlorë: Where Mountains Embrace the Sea

Picture a city where the mountains embrace the sea, and you'll find yourself in Vlorë. This coastal gem, situated on the Albanian Riviera, offers a harmonious blend of natural beauty and cultural richness.

Vlorë is not just a destination; it's a gateway to the stunning Albanian Riviera, known for its pristine beaches, crystal-clear waters, and charming coastal villages. Dive into the turquoise hues of the Ionian Sea and bask in the Mediterranean sun on the beaches of Dhërmi, Jale, and Himara.

The city itself boasts historical significance, with the Independence Monument standing tall as a symbol of Albania's declaration of independence in 1912. The Kaninë Castle, perched on a hill overlooking the city, provides panoramic views of the coastline.

Korca: The City of Serenades

Nestled in the southeastern part of Albania, Korça is a city known for its cultural richness, vibrant arts scene, and a distinct charm that earned it the nickname "The City of Serenades." Surrounded by rolling hills and vineyards, Korça exudes a relaxed atmosphere that resonates with both locals and visitors.

The Old Bazaar of Korça, with its Ottoman-era architecture, is a testament to the city's historical significance as a trade center. The Resurrection Cathedral, one of the largest Orthodox churches in the Balkans, dominates the skyline, reflecting the city's religious diversity.

Korça's cultural scene comes alive with events such as the Korça Beer Fest and the Serenata Festival, showcasing the city's love for music, arts, and celebration. The proximity to the Prespa National Park adds a touch of natural splendor to the city's allure.

Berat: The City of a Thousand Windows

In the heart of Albania, the city of Berat stands as a living testament to the country's cultural heritage. Known as the "City of a Thousand Windows," Berat's well-preserved Ottoman architecture and historic charm earned it a UNESCO World Heritage status.

Perched on the banks of the Osum River, Berat is divided into three distinct districts: the Kalaja (Castle) with its medieval fortress, the Mangalem quarter with its narrow streets and white Ottoman houses, and the Gorica quarter on the opposite riverbank.

Berat invites you to meander through its cobblestone streets, explore its museums, and savor the panoramic views from the castle. The Onufri Museum, housed within the castle, showcases a collection of medieval art, including the renowned works of Onufri, a celebrated Albanian icon painter.

The Decision-Making Process

As you navigate the diverse options for your destination in Albania, consider the following factors to guide your decision:

1. **Lifestyle Preferences:** Reflect on your lifestyle preferences, whether you're drawn to the dynamic urban life of Tirana, the coastal serenity of Vlorë, or the historical charm of Gjirokastër.

2. **Job Opportunities:** Explore the job market in your chosen destination. Tirana, as the capital, offers a plethora of professional opportunities, while other cities may cater to specific industries or sectors.

3. **Cultural Compatibility:** Consider the cultural nuances of each destination. Some cities may be more cosmopolitan, while others embrace a more traditional way of life. Align your preferences with the cultural vibe of the city.

4. **Cost of Living:** Evaluate the cost of living in each destination, factoring in accommodation, transportation, and everyday expenses. This will play a crucial role in determining the sustainability of your lifestyle in the chosen city.

5. **Outdoor and Recreational Opportunities:** If you're an outdoor enthusiast, consider the proximity of your chosen destination to natural attractions, hiking trails, and recreational activities. Albania's diverse landscapes offer a range of options for nature lovers.

6. **Community and Networking:** Explore the expatriate and local communities in each city. Building a network of friends and acquaintances will contribute to a more fulfilling

experience and provide a support system during your transition.

7. **Educational Facilities:** If you have children, research the educational facilities in your chosen destination. Consider the availability of international schools, language programs, and extracurricular activities.

8. **Healthcare Facilities:** Assess the healthcare infrastructure in each city. Ensure that your chosen destination has reliable medical facilities, hospitals, and access to essential healthcare services.

The Beauty of Options

The beauty of choosing your destination in Albania lies in the diversity of options that cater to a spectrum of lifestyles. Whether you're drawn to the bustling urban energy of Tirana, the historical allure of Gjirokastër, or the coastal tranquility of Vlorë, each destination offers a unique chapter in the story of your Albanian adventure.

As you contemplate your choice, let your heart guide you, but also let practical considerations shape your decision. Albania, with its tapestry of cities and regions, is ready to welcome you with open arms, each destination offering a canvas for you to paint the life you've envisioned.

So, take your time, explore the nuances of each city, and listen to the whispers of the Albanian landscapes. The choice of your destination is not just about where you'll live; it's about where you'll thrive, find inspiration, and embark on the next exciting chapter of your life. As you stand at the crossroads of possibilities, know that the beauty of Albania lies not just in its landscapes but in the diverse destinations that invite you to become part of their stories.

Chapter 4
Housing and Accommodation

As you step into the realm of relocation, finding a place to call home becomes a pivotal part of your journey. Housing and accommodation, beyond being a mere roof over your head, play a profound role in shaping your experience in a new country. In Albania, a land of diverse landscapes and vibrant cities, the options for housing are as varied as the destinations themselves. Whether you're drawn to the historical charm of traditional stone houses or the modern comforts of urban apartments, let's navigate the intricate world of housing in Albania—a place where your daily surroundings become the backdrop to your adventure.

Understanding the Housing Landscape

Before delving into the specifics, let's take a moment to understand the housing landscape in Albania. The country has experienced significant changes in recent decades, transitioning from a communist regime to a more open and dynamic society. This shift has influenced the housing market, creating a blend of traditional and modern options for residents and expatriates alike.

In urban centers like Tirana, you'll find a mix of apartment complexes, modern condominiums, and residential neighborhoods. The cityscape reflects the rapid development and growing infrastructure, with a range of housing options catering to diverse preferences.

In contrast, historic cities like Gjirokastër and Berat offer a glimpse into Albania's architectural heritage. Stone houses with tiled roofs line narrow cobblestone streets, creating a scene reminiscent of a bygone era. These cities, recognized as UNESCO World Heritage Sites, offer a unique opportunity to live within the walls of centuries-old structures.

For those seeking coastal living, cities like Vlorë and Himara on the Albanian Riviera boast a selection of apartments, villas, and beachfront properties. The coastline, with its azure waters and sun-drenched beaches, provides a captivating setting for those envisioning a life by the sea.

Renting in Albania: Practical Considerations

Renting is a common choice for expatriates and locals alike, offering flexibility and the opportunity to explore different neighborhoods before committing to a long-term investment. Here are some practical considerations when it comes to renting in Albania:

1. **Lease Agreements:** When entering into a lease agreement, carefully review the terms and conditions. Ensure that all details, including rent amount, duration, and responsibilities (such as utility payments), are clearly outlined. While some landlords may be fluent in English, having a local interpreter or seeking translations can provide additional clarity.

2. **Renting Costs:** The cost of renting can vary depending on factors such as location, size, and amenities. In Tirana, for instance, rental prices may be higher compared to smaller towns. It's advisable to research average rental costs in your desired location and budget accordingly.

3. **Utilities:** Understand which utilities are included in the rent and which you'll be responsible for. Common utilities include water, electricity, heating, and internet. Factor these costs into your budget to ensure a comprehensive understanding of your monthly expenses.

4. **Property Management:** Depending on the property, you may interact directly with the landlord or engage with a property management company. Understanding the management structure can impact the efficiency of addressing maintenance issues, repairs, and communication regarding the property.

5. **Furnished vs. Unfurnished:** Rental properties in Albania may be offered as furnished or unfurnished. Consider your preferences and needs when choosing between the

convenience of a fully furnished space and the opportunity to
personalize an unfurnished one.

6. **Security Deposits:** It's common for landlords to request a
    security deposit, usually equivalent to one or two months' rent,
    as a safeguard against potential damages. Ensure that the terms
    for refunding the deposit are clearly outlined in the lease
    agreement.

7. **Neighborhood Exploration:** Take the time to explore
    different neighborhoods and assess their suitability for your
    lifestyle. Consider factors such as proximity to amenities,
    public transportation, safety, and the overall vibe of the
    community.

Buying Property in Albania: A Long-Term Investment

For those considering a more permanent commitment, buying property in Albania is a viable option. The real estate market in the country
has witnessed increased interest from both locals and international buy-
ers. Here are key considerations for buying property:

1. **Legal Requirements:** Understand the legal requirements for
    purchasing property in Albania. Foreigners are generally
    permitted to buy real estate, but certain restrictions may apply
    in specific areas, such as near national borders.

2. **Property Title and Ownership:** Ensure that the property has
    clear title ownership and is free of any encumbrances. Engage
    the services of a reputable notary and legal professionals to
    navigate the intricacies of property transactions.

3. **Location and Infrastructure:** Assess the location of the
    property in terms of accessibility, infrastructure, and proximity
    to amenities. Whether you're drawn to the urban buzz of
    Tirana, the historical charm of Gjirokastër, or the coastal allure
    of Vlorë, each location offers a distinct living experience.

4. **Budgeting for Additional Costs:** In addition to the property

purchase price, budget for additional costs such as property taxes, notary fees, legal fees, and potential renovation or maintenance expenses. Having a comprehensive understanding of the financial implications will contribute to a well-informed decision.

5. **Engaging Local Real Estate Professionals:** Collaborate with local real estate professionals who have a deep understanding of the market. Real estate agents, lawyers, and notaries can provide invaluable guidance throughout the property-buying process.

6. **Market Trends and Property Values:** Stay informed about market trends and property values in your desired location. Conduct thorough research, attend property viewings, and engage in discussions with local experts to make informed decisions about your investment.

Traditional Homes and Modern Living

The architectural diversity in Albania is a delightful tapestry that weaves together tradition and modernity. Traditional homes, often found in historic cities like Gjirokastër and Berat, offer a unique living experience. Stone houses with wooden shutters, courtyard gardens, and tiled roofs create an ambiance that transports you to a different era. Living in a historic home provides not just shelter but an immersive journey through the cultural heritage of Albania.

On the flip side, urban centers like Tirana boast modern apartments and condominiums equipped with contemporary amenities. High-rise buildings, sleek designs, and proximity to commercial centers define the modern living experience in Albania's capital. For those seeking the comforts of city life, modern housing options provide a blend of convenience and style.

Navigating the Cultural Nuances of Housing

Understanding the cultural nuances of housing in Albania contributes to a smoother integration into your new community. Here are some cultural considerations:

1. **Hospitality of Landlords:** Albanians are known for their warm hospitality, and this extends to interactions with landlords. Building a positive relationship with your landlord can enhance your living experience. A genuine interest in local customs and respectful communication go a long way.

2. **Community Engagement:** In smaller towns and villages, community engagement is often an integral part of daily life. Embrace the opportunity to participate in local events, festivals, and community activities. Establishing connections with neighbors fosters a sense of belonging.

3. **Respect for Traditions:** If you choose to live in a traditional home, be mindful of the cultural and historical significance of the architecture. Respect for local traditions, such as maintaining the aesthetics of the exterior, contributes to the preservation of the community's heritage.

4. **Language of Communication:** While English is spoken in urban centers and tourist areas, learning basic Albanian phrases can enhance your communication with neighbors, landlords, and local businesses. The effort to speak the local language is often appreciated and fosters a sense of connection.

5. **Navigating Bureaucracy:** Navigating administrative processes related to housing may require patience and an understanding of local bureaucracy. Engaging local professionals for legal and administrative matters can streamline the process and ensure compliance with local regulations.

Embracing the Journey of Housing in Albania

Whether you opt for the urban buzz of Tirana, the historical charm of Gjirokastër, or the coastal serenity of Vlorë, your choice of housing in

Albania is an integral part of your journey. It's not just about finding a place to live; it's about immersing yourself in the daily rhythms of a new culture, forging connections with neighbors, and creating a home that resonates with your aspirations.

As you embark on the adventure of housing and accommodation, remember that each stone house, apartment balcony, or beachfront villa has a story to tell. It becomes a canvas upon which you paint the chapters of your Albanian experience. So, open the door to your new home with curiosity, embrace the cultural nuances, and let the journey of housing in Albania be a vibrant chapter in the unfolding narrative of your life.

Chapter 5
Settling In

The plane touched down on Albanian soil, and as you step onto the tarmac, a sense of anticipation mingles with the crisp air. The decision to relocate to Albania is not just about changing your address; it's a journey of transformation, of acclimating to a new rhythm and discovering the layers of a culture waiting to embrace you. Settling in is a nuanced dance that goes beyond unpacking boxes and finding your way around. It's about weaving your story into the vibrant tapestry of your new home, about forging connections, and about allowing the daily cadence of life to become your own. So, as you take the first steps on this new adventure, let's explore the art of settling in—the process of making Albania not just a destination but a place where you belong.

Navigating the First Days

The initial days of settling in are a delicate dance between excitement and the unknown. Whether you land in the bustling heart of Tirana, the historic charm of Gjirokastër, or the coastal serenity of Vlorë, the first order of business is to navigate the essentials. Find your bearings, explore your neighborhood, and let the daily rhythm of life unfold organically.

Take a leisurely stroll through the streets, pop into local cafes, and immerse yourself in the ebb and flow of daily life. The smell of strong Albanian coffee wafting from kafenes, the chatter of locals in the markets, and the distant echoes of call to prayer—all these sensory nuances are threads weaving you into the fabric of Albanian culture.

Connecting with the Local Community

One of the most enriching aspects of settling in is the opportunity to connect with the local community. Albanians are known for their warm hospitality and genuine curiosity about newcomers. Don't hesitate to strike up conversations with neighbors, shopkeepers, or fellow patrons at the local bakery. A simple "Tungjatjeta" (hello) and a warm smile can open doors to friendships that enhance your experience.

Engage in local events, festivals, and community gatherings. Albania's calendar is dotted with celebrations that offer a window into the cultural richness of the country. Whether it's the lively atmosphere of a traditional wedding or the festivities of a religious holiday, participating in these events provides a deeper understanding of the local way of life.

Consider joining local clubs, language exchange programs, or volunteering opportunities. This not only allows you to contribute to the community but also creates avenues for meaningful connections. The more you engage with the local community, the more Albania becomes not just a place you live but a place where you actively participate and contribute.

Embracing the Culinary Adventure

Albanian cuisine is a journey in itself—a delightful exploration of flavors, aromas, and traditions. Settling in is the perfect time to embark on a culinary adventure. Explore local markets, indulge in street food, and savor the rich tapestry of Albanian dishes.

Visit traditional kuzhinës (kitchens) and taste regional specialties. Whether it's the hearty flavors of tave kosi (baked lamb with yogurt) or the simplicity of byrek (savory pastry), each dish carries a story embedded in centuries of culinary heritage.

Engage with locals to learn cooking techniques, attend cooking classes, and bring the flavors of Albania into your own kitchen. Food is not just sustenance; it's a communal experience that fosters connections and creates shared memories.

Learning the Language

While many Albanians, especially in urban areas, speak English, taking the time to learn the local language adds a layer of connection and cultural immersion. Albanian, with its unique linguistic roots, may seem challenging at first, but the effort is greatly appreciated by locals.

Enroll in language classes, practice with language exchange partners, and embrace the journey of linguistic discovery. Beyond the practical benefits of navigating daily life, speaking Albanian opens doors to deeper interactions and a richer understanding of the culture.

Don't be afraid to make mistakes; locals often appreciate the effort and are eager to help you improve. Learning the language is not just about words; it's about embracing the nuances, idioms, and expressions that reflect the soul of Albania.

Navigating Practicalities: Services and Amenities

Settling in involves tackling the practicalities of daily life, from setting up utilities to finding essential services. Here are some key considerations:

1. **Utilities and Services:** Ensure that you've set up essential utilities such as water, electricity, and internet. Familiarize yourself with local service providers and payment procedures. Local shops and markets are also essential for day-to-day needs.

2. **Healthcare:** Register with local healthcare services and familiarize yourself with nearby clinics, hospitals, and pharmacies. If you have specific medical needs, ensure that you have access to the necessary facilities and medications.

3. **Transportation:** Explore local transportation options, whether it's public transit, taxis, or rental services. Understanding the local transportation system is key to navigating the city or region efficiently.

4. **Banking and Finances:** If you haven't already, set up a local bank account to facilitate financial transactions. Familiarize yourself with local banking practices, currency, and ATMs in your area.

5. **Education:** If you have children, explore educational options in your locality. Visit local schools, inquire about language programs, and understand the enrollment process. Connect

with other parents for insights into the education system.

6. **Cultural and Recreational Opportunities:** Delve into the cultural and recreational offerings of your new home. Attend local performances, visit museums, and explore natural attractions. Albania's diverse landscapes provide ample opportunities for outdoor activities.

Creating a Home Away from Home

Your dwelling is more than a place to sleep; it's your sanctuary, your refuge, and the canvas on which you paint the chapters of your Albanian adventure. Here are some tips for creating a home away from home:

1. **Personalizing Your Space:** Whether you're in a traditional stone house or a modern apartment, infuse your living space with personal touches. Bring mementos from your previous home, display artwork, and surround yourself with items that evoke a sense of familiarity.

2. **Exploring Local Markets:** Local markets are not just places to shop; they're cultural hubs. Explore markets for fresh produce, local crafts, and unique finds that add character to your home. Engage with local artisans and support the community.

3. **Seasonal Celebrations:** Embrace local celebrations and traditions, especially during holidays and festivals. Decorate your home in alignment with local customs, participate in festivities, and share the joy with neighbors.

4. **Connecting Virtually:** Stay connected with friends and family back home through virtual channels. Video calls, social media, and online platforms provide a bridge between your old and new lives. Share your experiences, exchange stories, and involve loved ones in your journey.

5. **Cultivating Hobbies:** Settling in is the perfect time to explore or cultivate hobbies. Whether it's joining a local sports club, attending art classes, or engaging in outdoor activities,

pursuing your passions creates a sense of fulfillment and connection.

Overcoming Challenges and Celebrating Milestones

Settling in is not without its challenges, and embracing the journey means acknowledging both the highs and lows. Language barriers, cultural differences, and the inevitable adjustment period are part of the process. Here are strategies for navigating challenges:

1. **Patience and Adaptability:** Cultivate patience and a spirit of adaptability. Understand that the initial period of adjustment is a natural part of the relocation process. Approach challenges with an open mind and a willingness to learn.

2. **Seeking Support:** Connect with local expatriate communities, seek support from new friends, and share experiences with fellow newcomers. Having a support system is invaluable during moments of uncertainty or homesickness.

3. **Mindful Self-Care:** Prioritize self-care as you navigate the intricacies of settling in. Whether it's taking walks, practicing mindfulness, or indulging in activities you enjoy, nurturing your well-being contributes to a positive settling-in experience.

4. **Celebrating Milestones:** Acknowledge and celebrate milestones, no matter how small. Whether it's successfully navigating public transportation, learning a new phrase in Albanian, or making your first local friend, each achievement is a step forward in your journey.

Embracing the Adventure

As you settle into your new life in Albania, remember that the adventure is not a destination but a continuous unfolding of experiences. It's in the laughter shared with neighbors, the aroma of Albanian cuisine wafting through your kitchen, and the moments of connection that transcend language.

Albania, with its warm-hearted people, rich history, and diverse landscapes, invites you to become part of its story. Settling in is not about erasing the traces of your past but about weaving them into the fabric of your present. So, open your heart to the rhythm of Albanian life, embrace the nuances, and let the journey of settling in be a tapestry of discovery, growth, and the beauty of a life well-lived. As you embark on this chapter, know that the best is yet to come—the unwritten pages of your Albanian adventure await, and they hold the promise of a home you'll cherish and a life enriched by the vibrant culture that surrounds you.

Chapter 6
Education and Schools

In the intricate mosaic of relocation, the chapter on education and schools is a pivotal page. For families embarking on the Albanian adventure, the prospect of finding the right educational environment for their children is a significant consideration. Albania, with its rich cultural heritage and evolving educational landscape, offers a tapestry of options for learners of all ages. Whether you're navigating the choices in Tirana, Gjirokastër, or Vlorë, the journey into Albanian education is a fusion of tradition and modernity—a canvas where young minds can flourish and explore the wonders of a new academic chapter.

The Educational Landscape in Albania

Understanding the educational landscape is a crucial starting point. Albania's education system has undergone significant transformations in recent years, transitioning from a centralized model to a more decentralized and diverse structure. The system encompasses various levels, including pre-school, primary, secondary, and higher education.

Pre-school Education: Laying the Foundation

For the youngest learners, pre-school education sets the foundation for future academic journeys. In Albania, pre-schools cater to children aged 3 to 6 and focus on early childhood development. These institutions provide a nurturing environment where children engage in activities that foster social skills, creativity, and basic cognitive abilities.

Pre-school education in Albania often incorporates play-based learning, arts and crafts, and early language acquisition. As a parent, exploring local pre-schools and understanding their curriculum, teaching philosophy, and facilities is essential. Many pre-schools in urban areas, especially Tirana, offer bilingual programs, easing the transition for international families.

Primary Education: Building Fundamental Skills

Primary education in Albania spans grades 1 to 9, with a focus on building fundamental skills in subjects such as language, mathematics, sciences, and social studies. The curriculum is designed to provide a well-rounded education and includes subjects like physical education, music, and arts.

Local primary schools follow the Albanian curriculum, and the language of instruction is Albanian. However, in larger cities and areas with expatriate communities, there are international schools that offer bilingual or English-medium programs. These schools often follow international curricula, such as the International Baccalaureate (IB) or Cambridge curriculum, providing a familiar academic structure for expatriate students.

When considering primary schools, it's essential to visit campuses, meet with educators, and inquire about extracurricular activities, support services, and the overall school culture. Many schools in Albania welcome parent involvement, creating a collaborative educational environment.

Secondary Education: Preparing for the Future

Secondary education in Albania covers grades 10 to 12 and represents a critical phase where students prepare for higher education or enter vocational training. The curriculum becomes more specialized, allowing students to delve deeper into subjects of interest and prepare for national exams.

In addition to the national secondary schools, international schools offer programs that lead to internationally recognized qualifications, such as the International General Certificate of Secondary Education (IGCSE) or the IB Diploma. These programs provide a global perspective and often facilitate a seamless transition for students moving between countries.

Considerations for secondary education include the availability of advanced courses, language of instruction, college counseling services, and extracurricular opportunities. Engaging with educators and exploring the school's track record in university placements are crucial aspects of the decision-making process.

Higher Education: Nurturing Academic Pursuits

Albania's higher education landscape has witnessed notable developments in recent years. The country is home to several universities and higher education institutions, offering a range of academic programs across disciplines. Tirana, the capital, hosts the majority of universities, attracting students from different parts of Albania and beyond.

International students exploring higher education options in Albania will find universities that offer programs in English, especially in fields such as business, engineering, and humanities. Admission requirements, application processes, and tuition fees vary, and prospective students should research individual universities for specific details.

As an expatriate family, understanding the higher education landscape is relevant not only for your children but also if you are considering pursuing academic endeavors or professional development opportunities.

International Schools: Bridging Cultures

For expatriate families, international schools play a significant role in providing an educational bridge between cultures. These schools offer curricula that follow international standards, allowing students to seamlessly transition between educational systems in different countries.

International schools in Albania, particularly in Tirana, provide an English-medium education with a global perspective. The curriculum often aligns with international standards, and some schools offer programs such as the IB or Cambridge curriculum. The advantage of international schools lies not only in the academic continuity they provide but also in the diverse cultural environment they cultivate.

When exploring international schools, consider factors such as accreditation, faculty qualifications, facilities, and the school's commitment to fostering a multicultural learning environment. Many international schools actively involve parents in the school community, creating a supportive network for expatriate families.

Language Considerations: Bilingual Education

Language is a central consideration for expatriate families navigating the Albanian education landscape. While many schools, especially in urban areas, offer bilingual or English-medium programs, the national language of instruction is Albanian.

For families seeking to integrate into the local education system, language acquisition becomes an important aspect. Language courses, language exchange programs, and immersion experiences can support both parents and students in developing proficiency in Albanian. The effort to learn the local language is often appreciated by the community and enhances the overall experience of living in Albania.

Navigating the School Selection Process

Navigating the school selection process involves a thoughtful exploration of options and a consideration of factors that align with your family's values and educational goals. Here are key steps in the school selection journey:

1. **Researching Schools:** Begin by researching schools in your area of residence. Consider factors such as curriculum, language of instruction, extracurricular activities, and the school's philosophy. Explore school websites, attend open houses, and gather information about each institution.

2. **Campus Visits:** Schedule visits to potential schools to get a firsthand experience of the campus environment. During visits, observe classrooms, meet with educators, and inquire about the school's approach to teaching and learning. Pay attention to the facilities, library, sports areas, and other amenities.

3. **Meeting with Educators:** Engage in conversations with school administrators, teachers, and support staff. Discuss the school's academic philosophy, teaching methodologies, and any specific

support services available for students. Understanding the school's commitment to student well-being and academic success is crucial.

4. **Exploring Extracurricular Opportunities:** Inquire about the range of extracurricular activities offered by the school. Whether it's sports, arts, music, or clubs, extracurricular engagement plays a significant role in a student's holistic development.

5. **Considering Commute and Accessibility:** Evaluate the practical aspects of school selection, including commute time, transportation options, and the overall accessibility of the school. Consider how the school's location aligns with your family's lifestyle and daily routines.

6. **Engaging with the School Community:** Connect with the school community, including other parents, to gain insights into the overall school experience. Attend parent-teacher meetings, school events, and community gatherings to foster connections and build a support network.

7. **Understanding Admission Procedures:** Familiarize yourself with the admission procedures for each school. Understand the documentation required, admission deadlines, and any entrance assessments or interviews. Ensure that you have a clear understanding of the tuition fees and any additional costs.

Supporting Your Child's Transition

The transition into a new school is a significant milestone for children. Whether they are entering pre-school, primary, or secondary education, providing support during this period contributes to a positive academic experience. Here are ways to support your child's transition:

1. **Open Communication:** Maintain open communication with your child about the upcoming changes. Discuss the new school, share information about the curriculum, and address

any concerns or questions they may have.

2. **School Familiarization:** Take your child for a visit to the new school before the academic year begins. Familiarize them with the campus, classrooms, and important areas such as the cafeteria and playground. Meeting teachers and school staff in advance can help alleviate anxiety.

3. **Establishing Routines:** Establish consistent routines at home to create a sense of stability. Set regular bedtimes, prepare school supplies together, and create a dedicated study area. Routines provide a sense of predictability during times of change.

4. **Connecting with Peers:** Encourage your child to connect with peers before the school year starts. Attend any orientation events or playdates organized by the school. Building friendships in advance can ease the social transition.

5. **Encouraging Independence:** Foster independence in your child by involving them in decisions related to school, such as choosing school supplies or a backpack. Encourage them to express their preferences and take ownership of their academic journey.

6. **Positive Reinforcement:** Focus on the positive aspects of the new school experience. Highlight exciting opportunities, interesting subjects, and potential friendships. Positive reinforcement helps create a mindset of optimism and curiosity.

Beyond Academics: Cultural Immersion

Education extends beyond the confines of the classroom—it is a holistic experience that encompasses cultural immersion, personal growth, and the development of a global perspective. For expatriate families in Albania, cultural immersion is an integral aspect of the educational journey.

Encourage your child to engage with local customs, traditions, and celebrations. Participate in cultural events, visit historical sites, and explore the rich tapestry of Albanian heritage. Language acquisition is not just a practical skill; it opens doors to deeper connections with the local community.

Schools, especially international ones, often incorporate cultural activities, language courses, and field trips that enhance students' understanding of the host country. Embrace these opportunities as a family, allowing education to extend beyond textbooks and classrooms.

Addressing Challenges and Celebrating Achievements

The educational journey is not without its challenges, and addressing them with resilience and collaboration is key. Here are strategies for navigating challenges and celebrating educational achievements:

1. **Communication with Educators:** Maintain open lines of communication with your child's teachers and school administrators. If challenges arise, collaborate with educators to find solutions and support strategies. Regular communication fosters a strong partnership between parents and the school.

2. **Support Networks:** Connect with other parents, both local and expatriate, to build a support network. Sharing experiences, insights, and resources creates a sense of community and solidarity. Attend parent-teacher meetings and engage in school activities to stay connected.

3. **Encouraging Adaptability:** Foster adaptability in your child by reinforcing the value of embracing new experiences. Encourage a positive attitude toward change, celebrate small achievements, and highlight the resilience developed through navigating diverse educational environments.

4. **Celebrating Cultural Diversity:** Celebrate cultural diversity within the school community. Organize cultural exchange

events, where students can share aspects of their cultural heritage. Embracing diversity creates an inclusive environment that enriches the educational experience for all.

5. **Balancing Academic and Cultural Exploration:** Strike a balance between academic pursuits and cultural exploration. While academic achievements are important, equally celebrate cultural discoveries, language milestones, and personal growth. Education is a multifaceted journey encompassing both intellectual and cultural dimensions.

A Chapter in Continuous Evolution

Education is a dynamic chapter in the book of relocation, one that unfolds gradually, shaping the narrative of personal and academic growth. Whether your child is embarking on the first day of pre-school, navigating the challenges of secondary education, or pursuing higher studies, the educational journey in Albania is a chapter in continuous evolution.

As you explore the diverse educational landscape, remember that the pages of this chapter are not just about grades and exams but about the friendships forged in school corridors, the excitement of discovery in science labs, and the moments of inspiration sparked in the classroom.

Albania, with its centuries-old history and contemporary vibrancy, offers a unique backdrop for this educational odyssey. Each lesson learned, every cultural exchange, and every achievement in the classroom become threads that weave into the rich tapestry of your child's educational journey.

So, as you navigate the choices, explore campuses, and witness your child's growth, know that the chapter on education is a story of exploration, resilience, and the beauty of learning in a new land. Embrace the evolving narrative, celebrate the milestones, and let the journey of education in Albania be a vibrant chapter in the unfolding narrative of your family's adventure.

Chapter 7
Employment Opportunities

The decision to relocate to Albania marks not just a change in scenery but often a shift in the professional landscape. As you set foot on this Balkan gem, the prospect of employment becomes a central part of your new narrative. Whether you're drawn to the vibrant capital of Tirana, the historic charm of Gjirokastër, or the coastal allure of Vlorë, Albania offers a diverse canvas for professional pursuits. The pages of this chapter unfold into a story of career exploration, cultural integration, and the potential for growth in a land where tradition and modernity coexist.

Understanding the Job Market in Albania

Before delving into the specifics of employment opportunities, let's take a panoramic view of the job market in Albania. The country has undergone significant economic transformations in recent decades, transitioning from a centrally planned economy to a market-oriented one. Today, Albania boasts a growing economy, especially in sectors such as tourism, information technology, energy, and agriculture.

Tirana, the capital and economic hub, is a melting pot of opportunities, with a burgeoning business scene, government institutions, and a dynamic expatriate community. Other cities, including Durrës, Vlorë, and Shkodër, also offer employment prospects, each with its unique charm and economic activities.

Navigating Employment Opportunities

1. **Language Skills:** While English is widely spoken, especially in urban areas and industries such as tourism and IT, having a grasp of the local language, Albanian, can enhance your professional interactions and open up additional opportunities. Consider taking language courses or engaging in language exchange programs to improve your language skills.

2. **Networking:** Building a professional network is a cornerstone of success in Albania. Attend industry events, conferences, and networking meet-ups to connect with professionals in your field. Expatriate and local business associations can be valuable resources for making connections and staying informed about job opportunities.

3. **Online Platforms:** Leverage online platforms for job searches and networking. Websites like LinkedIn, Glassdoor, and local job portals provide a platform to explore job opportunities, connect with employers, and showcase your professional profile. Joining relevant groups and forums can also offer insights and connections.

4. **Local Job Agencies:** Consider reaching out to local job agencies that specialize in recruitment for specific industries. These agencies often have insights into the current job market, can provide guidance on crafting a local-style resume, and may connect you with employers looking for your skill set.

5. **Entrepreneurship Opportunities:** Albania's entrepreneurial landscape is evolving, with opportunities for those looking to start their own businesses. Whether it's in the hospitality sector, technology startups, or niche markets, exploring entrepreneurial ventures can be a fulfilling path for those with a pioneering spirit.

6. **Consulting and Freelancing:** Many professionals find success in consulting or freelancing, offering their expertise on a project basis. This flexible approach allows you to navigate the market, build a client base, and contribute to various projects while maintaining a degree of autonomy.

Navigating Cultural Nuances in the Workplace

Understanding the cultural nuances of the Albanian workplace is essential for a smooth professional integration. Here are some considerations:

1. **Hierarchy and Respect:** Albanian workplaces often have a hierarchical structure, and respect for authority is highly valued. Addressing colleagues and superiors with proper titles and maintaining a respectful demeanor contribute to positive professional relationships.

2. **Business Etiquette:** Business etiquette in Albania places importance on personal relationships. Taking the time to engage in small talk, showing genuine interest in colleagues, and participating in social gatherings contribute to a positive work environment.

3. **Dress Code:** The dress code in Albanian workplaces is generally formal, especially in government institutions and corporate settings. Conservative and business-appropriate attire is the norm.

4. **Punctuality:** While punctuality is valued in professional settings, flexibility is also recognized. Meetings may start a bit later than scheduled, and a certain degree of adaptability to changes in plans is appreciated.

5. **Team Dynamics:** Building positive relationships with colleagues is crucial. Albanian workplaces often emphasize collaboration and a sense of camaraderie among team members.

Key Sectors and Industries

1. **Tourism and Hospitality:** Albania's tourism sector has experienced significant growth in recent years, making it a key contributor to the country's economy. Opportunities abound in hotels, restaurants, travel agencies, and related services.

Positions range from hospitality management to tour guiding and customer service.

2. **Information Technology:** The IT sector in Albania is expanding, with a focus on software development, cybersecurity, and IT services. Tirana, in particular, has emerged as a hub for tech companies, offering opportunities for software engineers, developers, and IT specialists.

3. **Energy and Infrastructure:** Infrastructure development and energy projects are significant contributors to Albania's economic growth. Opportunities exist in engineering, project management, renewable energy, and related fields. The government's focus on infrastructure improvements creates potential for professionals in construction and civil engineering.

4. **Agriculture and Agribusiness:** Agriculture plays a vital role in Albania, and the agribusiness sector offers opportunities in farming, food processing, and export. The country's fertile land and diverse climate create prospects for those interested in sustainable agriculture and agro-industrial activities.

5. **Language Teaching:** As the demand for language learning grows, there are opportunities for language teachers, especially in urban areas and language institutes. English, Italian, and other languages are in demand, and teaching positions can be found in schools, language centers, and private tutoring.

6. **Telecommunications:** The telecommunications sector is evolving, with opportunities for professionals in network management, telecommunications engineering, and technology infrastructure. Companies in this sector often seek skilled individuals to contribute to the expansion and improvement of communication networks.

Creating a Professional Identity in Albania

1. **Resume and CV:** Craft a resume that aligns with local expectations. Highlight relevant skills, experiences, and achievements. If possible, have your resume reviewed by a local professional or career advisor to ensure cultural alignment.

2. **Professional Development:** Continuous professional development is valued in Albania. Consider enrolling in local training programs, workshops, or conferences to enhance your skills and stay updated on industry trends.

3. **Embracing Flexibility:** The ability to adapt to changing circumstances and embrace flexibility is an asset in the Albanian professional landscape. Demonstrate your versatility and willingness to navigate dynamic work environments.

4. **Building Relationships:** Networking is a powerful tool in Albania. Attend industry events, join professional associations, and actively engage in networking opportunities. Building positive relationships with colleagues and industry peers contributes to your professional success.

5. **Showcasing Cultural Awareness:** Demonstrate cultural awareness and an understanding of Albanian customs and traditions. This can be reflected in your interactions with colleagues, clients, and superiors. Showcasing respect for the local culture enhances your professional image.

Entrepreneurship and Business Ownership

For those with an entrepreneurial spirit, Albania offers a canvas for business ownership and startup ventures. Whether it's in the hospitality sector, technology, agriculture, or niche markets, starting your own business allows you to contribute to the local economy and shape your professional journey.

1. **Research and Planning:** Conduct thorough research on the market and regulatory landscape. Understand the needs of the local community and identify gaps or opportunities that align

with your expertise.

2. **Legal and Regulatory Compliance:** Familiarize yourself with the legal and regulatory requirements for starting a business in Albania. This includes business registration, tax obligations, and any industry-specific regulations.

3. **Local Partnerships:** Building partnerships with local businesses, suppliers, and professionals can contribute to the success of your venture. Local knowledge and connections are valuable assets in navigating the business landscape.

4. **Community Engagement:** Engage with the local community and understand their needs. Building a business that aligns with local values and contributes to the well-being of the community fosters a positive reputation.

5. **Adaptability and Innovation:** The business landscape in Albania, like any other, requires adaptability and innovation. Stay informed about market trends, technological advancements, and changing consumer preferences to position your business for success.

Overcoming Challenges and Celebrating Milestones

The professional journey in Albania, like any relocation, comes with its share of challenges and triumphs. Here are strategies for navigating challenges and celebrating professional milestones:

1. **Cultural Adaptation:** Embrace the process of cultural adaptation. Understand that the Albanian workplace may have its unique dynamics, and adaptability is a valuable skill. Seek guidance from local colleagues and mentors to navigate cultural nuances.

2. **Language Learning:** Invest time in learning the local language. While English is widely spoken, having proficiency in Albanian enhances your ability to communicate effectively and fosters positive relationships in both professional and

social settings.

3. **Networking and Support:** Build a strong professional network and seek support from local and expatriate colleagues. Attend industry events, engage with professional associations, and actively participate in networking opportunities.

4. **Professional Development:** Prioritize professional development to stay competitive in your field. Attend workshops, conferences, and training programs to enhance your skills and contribute to your industry.

5. **Resilience and Persistence:** The journey of employment in a new country may have its ups and downs. Approach challenges with resilience and persistence. Celebrate small victories, learn from setbacks, and maintain a positive outlook on your professional journey.

Closing Thoughts: Your Professional Odyssey

As you embark on the chapter of employment in Albania, view it as an odyssey—a journey of professional exploration, cultural integration, and personal growth. The opportunities are diverse, the landscape is dynamic, and the potential for building a fulfilling career is vast.

Whether you find yourself in the bustling offices of Tirana, the entrepreneurial ventures of Shkodër, or the emerging industries of Vlorë, remember that your professional odyssey is not just about the tasks on your desk but about the relationships you forge, the cultural nuances you embrace, and the impact you make in the vibrant tapestry of the Albanian workplace.

So, open your professional heart to the opportunities that await, navigate the challenges with resilience, and let your journey in the Albanian workforce be a chapter of growth, connection, and the exciting promise of a career well-lived in the heart of the Balkans. As you turn the pages of this chapter, know that each day is a new opportunity to contribute to the unfolding narrative of your professional odyssey in Albania.

Chapter 8
Language and Communication

In the symphony of cultural experiences that is relocating to Albania, language is the melody that connects you to the heart of the nation. As you step into this land of contrasts, where ancient traditions harmonize with modern aspirations, embracing the Albanian language becomes a key to unlocking the richness of your journey. Language is not just a tool for communication; it is a bridge to understanding, a passport to deeper connections, and an invitation to be part of the vibrant tapestry of Albanian life.

The Melody of Albanian: A Linguistic Prelude

Albanian, with its melodic sounds and unique linguistic features, is a testament to the country's rich cultural heritage. Classified as an Indo-European language, Albanian stands as a linguistic outlier with no direct relatives, making it a linguistic gem that reflects the nation's distinct identity.

The Albanian language has two main dialects: Gheg in the north and Tosk in the south. While both dialects share a common core, regional variations add nuances to pronunciation, vocabulary, and expressions. As you embark on your linguistic journey, you'll encounter the warm embrace of the language, its intricate grammar, and the joy of learning expressions that mirror the soul of the Albanian people.

Navigating the Linguistic Landscape

1. **Learning the Basics:** As you settle into your new home, acquaint yourself with essential phrases and expressions. Simple greetings, polite phrases, and everyday words create a foundation for effective communication. Albanians appreciate the effort of foreigners learning their language, and even a few words can open doors and hearts.

Mirëdita! (Good day!)
Faleminderit. (Thank you.)
Ju lutem. (Please.)
Po/Jo. (Yes/No.)

1. **Language Courses:** Consider enrolling in language courses to deepen your understanding of Albanian. Language schools and institutes in urban areas, especially Tirana, offer courses for beginners and advanced learners. Engaging with a tutor or participating in group classes provides structured learning and opportunities for practice.

2. **Language Exchange:** Language exchange programs are a fantastic way to enhance your language skills while building connections with locals. This reciprocal learning approach allows you to teach your native language while learning Albanian from a language partner. It's a cultural exchange that goes beyond words.

3. **Mobile Apps and Online Resources:** Language-learning apps and online resources cater to various proficiency levels. Platforms like Duolingo, Babbel, and Memrise offer interactive lessons and exercises. Additionally, online dictionaries and language forums can be valuable references for expanding your vocabulary.

4. **Immersive Experiences:** Immerse yourself in the language by engaging in everyday activities. Whether it's shopping at local markets, dining in traditional restaurants, or participating in community events, these immersive experiences provide practical opportunities to apply your language skills and connect with locals.

The Art of Conversation: Cultural Nuances in Communication

1. **Warmth and Hospitality:** Albanians are known for their

warmth and hospitality, and this is reflected in their communication style. Conversations often include friendly gestures, eye contact, and a genuine interest in the well-being of others. Expect to be welcomed with open arms and engaging conversations.

2. **Non-Verbal Communication:** Non-verbal cues play a significant role in Albanian communication. Facial expressions, hand gestures, and body language convey nuances of meaning. A nod or a smile can express agreement, while subtle gestures may convey cultural understanding. Paying attention to these cues enhances your ability to connect with others.

3. **Formality and Informality:** The level of formality in Albanian communication depends on factors such as age, social status, and the nature of the relationship. While formal language may be used in professional settings or when addressing elders, informal language is common among peers and friends. Observing these nuances contributes to effective communication.

4. **Expressions of Politeness:** Politeness is deeply ingrained in Albanian culture. Using polite expressions, showing respect to elders, and using proper titles contribute to positive interactions. Expressions such as *Ju lutem* (please) and *Faleminderit* (thank you) are essential elements of courteous communication.

Building Bridges Across Languages: Multilingual Albania

While Albanian is the official language, you'll find a multilingual landscape shaped by historical influences, geographical proximity, and the country's openness to cultural diversity. Here are some linguistic dimensions that add vibrancy to the tapestry of communication:

1. **English:** English is widely spoken in urban areas, especially among the younger population, professionals, and those in the

tourism industry. In Tirana and other major cities, you'll find that many people have a good command of English, making communication accessible for expatriates.

2. **Italian and Greek:** Due to historical ties, geographic proximity, and migration patterns, Italian and Greek are languages with a notable presence in Albania. In coastal areas, you may encounter individuals who are fluent in Italian, and Greek is spoken in communities with Greek heritage.

3. **Bilingualism:** In regions with diverse linguistic influences, bilingualism is common. Many Albanians grow up learning both Gheg and Tosk dialects, showcasing the linguistic versatility that reflects the country's historical and cultural tapestry.

Navigating Workplaces and Social Settings

1. **Workplace Communication:** In professional settings, the language of communication depends on the nature of the workplace and the industry. While English is prevalent in international companies and tech-oriented environments, knowledge of Albanian is an asset for effective collaboration and integration into the workplace culture.

2. **Social Etiquette:** Engaging in social settings involves a blend of linguistic and cultural awareness. Whether attending gatherings, celebrations, or community events, participating in conversations and understanding cultural nuances contribute to a positive social experience.

3. **Learning from Locals:** One of the most enriching aspects of language acquisition is learning from locals. Strike up conversations with neighbors, colleagues, and community members. Sharing stories, asking about local customs, and expressing genuine interest in the language fosters connections and cultural understanding.

4. **Language and Identity:** Language is a key element of identity, and expressing interest in learning Albanian is a gesture that resonates with locals. Embracing the language is not just a practical skill but a way of signaling your commitment to understanding and integrating into the cultural fabric of Albania.

Celebrating Language Milestones

1. **Small Achievements:** Celebrate small language milestones as you progress in your learning journey. Whether it's successfully ordering food in Albanian, engaging in a brief conversation, or understanding a local joke, these achievements mark your linguistic growth and contribute to a sense of accomplishment.
2. **Language Events:** Attend language-related events, such as language meet-ups, cultural gatherings, or language exchange programs. These events provide opportunities to practice your skills, meet fellow language learners, and immerse yourself in the linguistic diversity of Albania.
3. **Cultural Integration:** Language is a gateway to cultural integration. As you learn Albanian, you gain insights into local customs, traditions, and ways of thinking. Engaging with the language enhances your ability to navigate diverse cultural landscapes and build meaningful connections.
4. **Language Challenges:** Embrace language challenges as part of the learning process. From navigating linguistic nuances to expanding your vocabulary, each challenge is a stepping stone toward fluency. Seek support from language tutors, fellow learners, and local friends to overcome obstacles and continue progressing.

Closing Thoughts: The Poetry of Connection

As you traverse the linguistic landscapes of Albania, remember that language is not just a means of communication; it is the poetry of connection, the art of understanding, and the soul of cultural integration. Embrace the journey of learning Albanian with curiosity, celebrate the diverse linguistic tapestry that colors the country, and let the words you speak become threads in the intricate fabric of your Albanian adventure.

In the realm of language and communication, every word learned is a step toward deeper connections, and every conversation is a verse in the poetry of cross-cultural understanding. So, let the melodies of Albanian fill your days, engage in the dance of words with locals, and savor the joy of expressing yourself in the language that echoes through the heart of this captivating nation. May your linguistic journey in Albania be a chapter of discovery, connection, and the beautiful artistry of language that binds us all.

Chapter 9
Making Friends and Building a Social Circle

In the unfolding story of your relocation to Albania, the chapter on making friends and building a social circle is a vibrant narrative of connection, shared experiences, and the warmth of human relationships. As you step into this new chapter of your life, the people you meet, the friendships you cultivate, and the communities you become a part of will shape the cultural tapestry of your Albanian adventure.

The Tapestry of Albanian Hospitality

Albania is renowned for its hospitality, and the warmth of its people creates a welcoming environment for newcomers. Making friends in Albania is not just about socializing; it's an invitation to share in the richness of local traditions, explore the nuances of daily life, and build connections that go beyond geographical borders.

Embracing Openness and Approachability

One of the hallmarks of Albanian culture is the approachability of its people. Whether you find yourself in the buzzing streets of Tirana or the quaint corners of Shkodër, don't be surprised if locals strike up conversations or extend invitations. Embrace the openness with a friendly smile, engage in small talk, and be receptive to the genuine warmth that defines Albanian interactions.

Navigating Social Settings and Cultural Nuances

1. **Coffee Culture:** Coffee is more than a beverage in Albania; it's a social ritual. From bustling cafés in city centers to tranquil spots along the coast, the culture of enjoying coffee is deeply ingrained. Invitations for coffee are common, and accepting such invitations provides a relaxed setting for conversations and getting to know people.

2. **Celebrations and Festivals:** Albanians love to celebrate, and participating in local festivals and celebrations is a fantastic way to immerse yourself in the community. Whether it's traditional music festivals, religious celebrations, or national holidays, these events offer opportunities to connect with locals and experience the vibrancy of Albanian culture.

3. **Community Events:** Keep an eye out for community events, art exhibitions, and cultural gatherings. Participating in these events introduces you to like-minded individuals and provides a platform to share interests. Local expatriate groups and community organizations often organize such events, creating spaces for socializing.

4. **Language Exchange:** Language exchange programs serve a dual purpose—improving language skills while building friendships. Engage with language exchange partners, whether through formal programs or informal arrangements. Beyond language, these interactions foster cross-cultural understanding and connection.

Navigating Expat and Local Circles

1. **Expat Communities:** Expatriate communities in Albania are diverse and welcoming. Whether you're in Tirana, Vlorë, or any other expatriate hub, joining expat groups provides an immediate social network. Attend expat meet-ups, social events, and gatherings to connect with individuals who share the experience of living in a new country.

2. **Local Connections:** Balancing expat circles with local connections enriches your social experience. Engage with neighbors, colleagues, and community members. Attend local events, support neighborhood initiatives, and take part in everyday activities to foster connections with Albanians.

3. **Social Media Groups:** Online platforms, especially social

media groups, play a significant role in connecting expatriates and locals. Joining groups related to your interests, hobbies, or specific locations allows you to interact with a diverse community and stay informed about local happenings.

Building Friendships: A Gradual Unfolding

1. **Patience and Consistency:** Building friendships takes time, and it's a process that unfolds gradually. Be patient, consistent, and open to the organic development of connections. Attend social gatherings regularly, engage in conversations, and allow friendships to evolve naturally.
2. **Shared Activities:** Shared activities create bonding opportunities. Whether it's joining a sports club, art class, or hiking group, participating in activities aligned with your interests introduces you to individuals with similar passions. The shared experience becomes a foundation for lasting friendships.
3. **Invitations and Reciprocity:** Accept invitations graciously, and reciprocate the gesture by extending your own invitations. Hosting a casual dinner, organizing a movie night, or planning a weekend outing provides a platform for deeper connections and strengthens the bonds of friendship.
4. **Cultural Exchange:** Embrace cultural exchange as a bridge to understanding. Share aspects of your own culture, and express genuine interest in learning about Albanian customs and traditions. Creating a cultural exchange fosters a sense of mutual respect and appreciation.

Overcoming Language Barriers

Navigating friendships in a new country may involve overcoming language barriers, and in Albania, the official language is Albanian. While many Albanians, especially in urban areas, speak English, making an effort to learn basic phrases in Albanian is appreciated. Language becomes a tool for deeper connection, and locals often respond warmly to the initiative of learning their language.

Celebrating Diversity in Friendship

Albania's history is a tapestry woven with diverse influences, and its people reflect this rich heritage. Friendships in Albania may include individuals from different backgrounds, religions, and ethnicities. Embrace the diversity of your social circle, appreciate the unique perspectives each friend brings, and celebrate the richness of a multicultural friendship.

Addressing Loneliness and Seeking Support

The journey of relocation may, at times, bring moments of loneliness. It's essential to acknowledge these feelings and seek support when needed. Whether through local counseling services, expatriate support groups, or online forums, reaching out to others who have experienced similar emotions fosters a sense of understanding and community.

Navigating the Dynamics of Local Friendships

1. **Family Bonds:** Family holds a central place in Albanian culture, and friendships often extend to family relationships. Invitations to family gatherings, celebrations, and shared meals are common. Embrace these invitations as opportunities to deepen connections and experience the warmth of Albanian hospitality.

2. **Reciprocal Support:** Albanians value reciprocal support in friendships. Offering assistance when needed, celebrating achievements, and providing a listening ear during challenges contribute to the depth of friendships. The concept of *burrneshëri* (solidarity among friends) reflects the strong bonds formed in Albanian friendships.

3. **Expressions of Affection:** Albanians are expressive in their friendships, often using gestures, hugs, and terms of endearment to convey affection. Embracing these cultural

expressions fosters a sense of closeness and emphasizes the importance of emotional connection in relationships.

Friendships and the Albanian Lifestyle

1. **Socializing in Cafés and Restaurants:** Cafés and restaurants are central to social life in Albania. Whether it's enjoying a leisurely coffee, savoring traditional Albanian cuisine, or exploring international flavors, these settings provide an ideal backdrop for socializing and spending time with friends.
2. **Weekend Getaways:** The diverse landscapes of Albania offer opportunities for weekend getaways. From the scenic Albanian Riviera to the historic charm of Gjirokastër, planning trips with friends allows you to explore the beauty of the country together and create lasting memories.
3. **Festivals and Events:** Joining friends in celebrating festivals, events, and local traditions enhances your cultural experience. Whether it's dancing at a music festival, participating in religious celebrations, or attending community events, these shared moments become integral to the fabric of your friendships.

Addressing Challenges in Friendships

Friendships, like any relationship, may encounter challenges. Cultural differences, communication nuances, or personal adjustments can be part of the journey. Addressing challenges with open communication, empathy, and a willingness to understand different perspectives contributes to the resilience of friendships.

Navigating the Dynamics of Expatriate Friendships

1. **Shared Experiences:** Expatriate friendships are often built on shared experiences of navigating life in a new country. Whether it's discovering local markets, overcoming language challenges,

or celebrating cultural milestones, these shared moments create a unique bond among expatriate friends.

2. **Support Network:** Expatriate communities often serve as support networks, providing assistance, guidance, and a sense of familiarity. Engaging in expat groups, attending social events, and participating in forums create opportunities to connect with individuals who understand the nuances of expatriate life.

3. **Cultural Exchange Among Expatriates:** Expatriate friendships offer a platform for cultural exchange among individuals from various backgrounds. Sharing stories, customs, and traditions from your home country and learning about the diverse experiences of others contribute to a rich tapestry of cultural understanding.

Celebrating Milestones in Friendships

1. **Anniversaries and Special Occasions:** Celebrate the anniversaries of friendships, birthdays, and special occasions with friends. Whether through a heartfelt message, a small gift, or organizing a gathering, acknowledging milestones fosters a sense of appreciation and strengthens the bonds of friendship.

2. **Creating Traditions:** Establishing traditions with friends adds a meaningful layer to your social circle. Whether it's a monthly dinner, an annual trip, or a shared hobby, creating traditions provides a sense of continuity and anticipation, contributing to the longevity of friendships.

3. **Navigating Transitions Together:** The journey of relocation involves transitions, and navigating these changes with friends creates a sense of support and continuity. Whether it's adjusting to a new job, moving to a different city, or adapting to cultural nuances, having friends by your side adds resilience to your journey.

Closing Thoughts: A Chapter of Connection

As you turn the pages of the chapter on making friends and building a social circle in Albania, remember that each interaction, each shared moment, and each friendship is a brushstroke in the portrait of your Albanian adventure. Embrace the diversity of connections, celebrate the cultural tapestry that unfolds around you, and let the friendships you cultivate become a source of joy, support, and shared laughter.

In the heart of Albania, where hospitality is a way of life and warmth is extended to newcomers, your social circle becomes a reflection of the inclusive spirit that defines this nation. So, step into the tapestry of Albanian friendships with an open heart, share in the experiences that unfold, and let the connections you make be a chapter of genuine connection, camaraderie, and the enduring beauty of human relationships.

Chapter 10
Exploring Albania

In the heart of the Balkans lies a hidden gem waiting to be discovered—the captivating land of Albania. As you embark on this chapter of exploration, prepare to be enchanted by a country that seamlessly weaves together ancient history, natural wonders, and vibrant contemporary life. From the rugged peaks of the Accursed Mountains to the pristine beaches along the Albanian Riviera, every corner of this diverse nation invites you on a journey of discovery, adventure, and cultural immersion.

A Tapestry of Landscapes: From Mountains to Coast

Albania's landscape is a masterpiece painted with diverse strokes, each region offering a unique tableau of natural beauty. Begin your exploration in the north, where the Accursed Mountains, or the Albanian Alps, beckon with their rugged peaks and pristine wilderness. This majestic range is a haven for hikers and nature enthusiasts, boasting trails that lead to panoramic vistas, hidden waterfalls, and remote villages where time seems to stand still.

As you venture southward, the landscape transforms into rolling hills, fertile valleys, and historic towns. The city of Shkodër, with its centuries-old castle and the tranquil waters of Lake Shkodra, offers a glimpse into Albania's rich history and natural splendor. Explore the cobbled streets, visit local markets, and embrace the serenity of this northern jewel.

Descending toward the Adriatic and Ionian coasts, you'll discover the Albanian Riviera—a stretch of coastline renowned for its pristine beaches, turquoise waters, and charming villages. Dive into the vibrant beach scene in Dhërmi, explore the secluded coves of Ksamil, and savor the coastal allure of Vlorë. The Riviera is a sun-drenched canvas inviting you to unwind, bask in the Mediterranean glow, and immerse yourself in the laid-back rhythm of seaside life.

Cultural Treasures: Ancient Cities and UNESCO Heritage

Albania's history is etched in the stone of its ancient cities and cultural landmarks. Tirana, the capital, is a dynamic fusion of tradition and modernity. Stroll through Skanderbeg Square, where the National History Museum and Et'hem Bey Mosque stand as testaments to the country's rich heritage. The vibrant Blloku district, once off-limits during the communist era, now pulses with trendy cafés, boutiques, and a lively atmosphere.

Journey back in time to the city of Gjirokastër, a UNESCO World Heritage site known for its well-preserved Ottoman architecture. The imposing Gjirokastër Castle, perched on a hill, offers panoramic views of the city and the surrounding mountains. Wander through the cobbled streets, visit the Skenduli House, and explore the unique charm of this historical gem.

In Berat, another UNESCO-listed city, you'll encounter a living museum of architecture. The well-preserved Ottoman houses, clustered on the hillside, create a breathtaking panorama known as the "City of a Thousand Windows." Stroll along the river, explore the castle perched above the town, and witness the convergence of history and contemporary life in this cultural oasis.

Nature's Palette: Lakes, Rivers, and National Parks

Albania's natural beauty extends beyond its mountains and coastline to embrace lakes, rivers, and national parks. Lake Ohrid, shared with North Macedonia, is a UNESCO World Heritage site and one of Europe's oldest and deepest lakes. The town of Pogradec, nestled along the lake's shore, provides a tranquil retreat with its lakeside promenade and panoramic views.

The Osumi River, cutting through the spectacular Osumi Canyon, offers a thrilling adventure for nature enthusiasts. Rafting along its winding course unveils the dramatic cliffs and lush landscapes that make this natural wonder a hidden treasure.

For those seeking an immersion in pristine wilderness, the Llogara Pass and the Vjosa-Narta Protected Landscape beckon. The Llogara Pass, with its winding road offering breathtaking vistas of the Ionian Sea, is a gateway to the lush landscapes of the Ceraunian Mountains. The Vjosa-Narta Protected Landscape, encompassing the Vjosa River and the Narta Lagoon, is a haven for birdwatching, kayaking, and exploring the rich biodiversity of southern Albania.

Culinary Odyssey: A Tantalizing Tapestry of Flavors

Albanian cuisine is a delectable journey that mirrors the country's diverse landscapes and cultural influences. From the hearty mountain fare to the coastal delights, each region contributes to a culinary tapestry that's both flavorful and unique.

In the north, indulge in traditional dishes like *flija*, a layered pancake, and *tave kosi*, a baked lamb and yogurt casserole. The mountainous regions are also known for their dairy products, including artisanal cheeses that showcase the pastoral traditions of the area.

As you venture southward, savor the seafood delights of the Albanian Riviera. Freshly caught fish, grilled octopus, and *tavë krapri* (baked carp) tantalize the taste buds, accompanied by local olive oil and the warmth of Mediterranean flavors. Coastal towns like Himara and Saranda offer an array of seafood restaurants where you can savor the catch of the day while overlooking the azure waters.

Tirana, with its burgeoning food scene, presents a fusion of traditional Albanian dishes and international flavors. Explore the city's diverse restaurants, trendy cafés, and street food stalls, where you can sample everything from *byrek* (savory pastry) to international cuisines.

Connecting with Locals: Festivals, Markets, and Everyday Life

To truly experience the heartbeat of Albania, immerse yourself in the tapestry of everyday life. Engage with locals at bustling markets like the Pazari i Ri in Tirana, where vendors showcase fresh produce, local crafts, and the vibrant energy of daily commerce. Bargain for souvenirs, taste local delicacies, and absorb the lively atmosphere of these cultural hubs.

Participate in traditional festivals that celebrate Albania's rich heritage. The Summer Day festivities in Gjirokastër, the Kala Festival in Durrës, and the National Folk Festival in Gjirokastër offer glimpses into the country's music, dance, and artistic traditions. Join in the celebrations, witness colorful parades, and let the rhythm of Albanian folklore envelop you.

For a deeper connection with local life, consider volunteering or attending community events. Albanians are known for their warmth and hospitality, and joining in communal activities provides opportunities to forge meaningful connections. Whether it's contributing to local initiatives, attending neighborhood gatherings, or participating in cultural workshops, these experiences offer a window into the soul of the Albanian community.

Off the Beaten Path: Hidden Gems and Untouched Landscapes

While popular destinations showcase the beauty of Albania, there are hidden gems and untouched landscapes awaiting the intrepid traveler. The village of Theth, nestled in the Albanian Alps, is a haven for hikers and nature lovers. Accessible by a scenic journey through the Theth National Park, this remote village offers a serene escape surrounded by mountain peaks and alpine meadows.

The Blue Eye (Syri i Kalter), a natural spring near Saranda, is a mesmerizing natural wonder. With its crystal-clear waters and vibrant blue hues, this spring is a tranquil oasis that invites contemplation and relaxation.

For a journey through time, explore the ancient city of Butrint, a UNESCO World Heritage site. Located near Saranda, Butrint boasts archaeological remains that span from the Greek and Roman periods to the Byzantine and Venetian eras. Wander through the well-preserved amphitheater, Roman baths, and ancient walls to witness the layers of history embedded in this archaeological gem.

Outdoor Adventures: Hiking, Beaches, and Beyond

Albania's diverse landscapes create a playground for outdoor enthusiasts. Hiking trails crisscross the country, offering experiences for all levels of adventurers. Explore the Valbona Valley in the Accursed Mountains, trek to the summit of Mount Dajti overlooking Tirana, or embark on the Peaks of the Balkans trail for a cross-border hiking odyssey.

The Albanian Riviera beckons beach lovers with its pristine shores and turquoise waters. Dhërmi, Jale, and Ksamil are just a few of the coastal havens where you can unwind on sandy beaches, snorkel in clear waters, and savor the Mediterranean sun.

For adrenaline seekers, the Llogara Pass presents paragliding opportunities with panoramic views of the Ionian Sea. The Vjosa River, one of Europe's last wild rivers, offers kayaking adventures through its scenic canyons and rapids. Whether you're a thrill-seeker or a nature lover, Albania's outdoor offerings cater to a spectrum of interests.

Practical Tips for Exploration: From Transportation to Cultural Etiquette

1. **Transportation:** Albania's transportation network includes buses, furgons (shared minivans), and taxis. Renting a car provides flexibility for exploring remote areas. Be prepared for mountainous roads and consider public transportation for city travel.
2. **Currency:** The official currency is the Albanian lek (ALL). Credit cards are widely accepted in urban areas, but cash is preferred in rural regions.
3. **Language:** Albanian is the official language, but English is commonly spoken in tourist areas and urban centers. Learning basic Albanian phrases enhances your travel experience and fosters local connections.
4. **Accommodation:** Albania offers a range of accommodations, from boutique hotels to guesthouses and beachfront resorts.

Book accommodations in advance during peak seasons.

5. **Cultural Etiquette:** Albanians are known for their hospitality. Greetings involve a firm handshake, and it's customary to bring a small gift when invited to someone's home. Express appreciation for local customs and traditions.

6. **Safety:** Albania is generally safe for travelers. Exercise standard safety precautions, avoid isolated areas at night, and be aware of traffic conditions, especially in mountainous regions.

7. **Weather:** Albania experiences a Mediterranean climate, with hot summers and mild winters. Coastal areas have a Mediterranean climate, while mountain regions may have cooler temperatures.

8. **Responsible Travel:** Respect local customs and the environment. Leave natural areas as you found them, support local businesses, and engage in responsible tourism practices.

Closing Thoughts: Your Albanian Odyssey

As you navigate the diverse landscapes, cultural treasures, and everyday life of Albania, remember that this chapter of exploration is an ongoing odyssey—a tapestry of experiences waiting to be woven into the fabric of your memories. From the majestic peaks of the north to the sun-kissed beaches of the south, every step reveals a new facet of this captivating nation.

So, let the mountain trails guide you, the coastal breezes embrace you, and the cultural wonders enchant you. Whether you're savoring the flavors of Albanian cuisine, celebrating with locals at a traditional festival, or discovering hidden gems off the beaten path, your exploration of Albania is a journey of discovery, connection, and the enduring allure of a land rich in history and natural splendor.

As you turn the pages of this chapter, let each adventure be a brushstroke in the canvas of your Albanian odyssey. Whether you find yourself atop a mountain summit, strolling through ancient streets, or simply sipping coffee in a bustling square, know that every moment is a stroke in the masterpiece of your exploration—an exploration that transcends geography and becomes a part of your personal narrative, forever etched in the captivating story of your journey through Albania.

Conclusion

A Tapestry of Memories - Embracing Your Albanian Adventure

As you reach the final pages of this guide to relocating and exploring Albania, you find yourself at the precipice of a conclusion, standing at the intersection of experiences, memories, and the rich tapestry of your Albanian journey. It's a moment to reflect on the chapters that have unfolded—the preface that sparked curiosity, the introduction that set the stage, the practicalities of relocation, the intricacies of language and connection, the friendships forged, and the landscapes explored. Each page turned is a chapter of growth, discovery, and the unique beauty that is Albania.

Reflecting on Relocation: A Beginning and an End

Your decision to relocate to Albania marked the beginning of a profound adventure—a journey not just across geographical borders but into the heart of a nation that embraces both its ancient roots and the vibrant pulse of contemporary life. The process of relocation, from planning your move to settling into a new home, is a testament to your resilience, adaptability, and the courage to embrace the unknown.

In the chapters dedicated to relocation, you navigated the intricacies of paperwork, sought housing that resonated with your lifestyle, and embraced the warmth of Albanian hospitality. The challenges and triumphs of this process have woven into the fabric of your experience, becoming threads in the story of resilience and the pursuit of a life filled with new possibilities.

The Dance of Language and Connection: A Cultural Symphony

Language became your guide in the symphony of cultural connection. As you delved into the nuances of Albanian, from basic greetings to the poetry of conversation, you discovered the power of language to bridge gaps, forge friendships, and immerse yourself in the soul of a nation. The chapter on language and communication unfolded as a dance—a rhythmic exchange of words, expressions, and the shared joy of understanding.

Whether you engaged in language exchange programs, enrolled in courses, or simply navigated everyday interactions, each conversation became a verse in the poetry of connection. The language you embraced became more than a tool; it became a reflection of your commitment to understanding and integrating into the cultural fabric of Albania.

Friendships as Anchors: A Tapestry of Connections

In the chapter on making friends and building a social circle, you stepped into the vibrant tapestry of Albanian friendships. The warmth of locals, the shared moments with fellow expatriates, and the diverse connections you cultivated became anchors in your journey. From coffee culture to community events, each interaction became a stroke in the canvas of your social landscape.

As you celebrated milestones, navigated cultural nuances, and forged connections that transcended language barriers, you discovered the universal language of friendship—the language of shared laughter, support, and the enduring beauty of human connections. Whether in bustling city centers or tranquil villages, your social circle became a reflection of the inclusive spirit that defines Albania.

Exploring the Kaleidoscope of Albania: An Ongoing Odyssey

The chapter on exploring Albania unveiled a kaleidoscope of landscapes, cultural treasures, and outdoor adventures. From the peaks of the Accursed Mountains to the pristine beaches of the Albanian Riviera, you journeyed through a diverse canvas that spoke of ancient history, natural wonders, and the allure of contemporary life.

Your culinary odyssey became a journey of flavors, a sensory exploration that mirrored the diverse landscapes of the country. From the heartiness of mountain fare to the seafood delights of the coast, each dish became a palate-pleasing revelation, inviting you to savor the richness of Albanian cuisine.

As you delved into the cultural tapestry of festivals, markets, and everyday life, you witnessed the heartbeat of Albania. Engaging with locals, participating in community events, and immersing yourself in the vibrant rhythm of daily life became integral to your exploration. Hidden gems, off-the-beaten-path wonders, and the outdoor adventures that unfolded expanded your understanding of the multifaceted beauty that is Albania.

Practical Wisdom: Navigating Your Albanian Journey

Throughout this guide, practical wisdom has accompanied you—an invaluable companion on your Albanian journey. From understanding the nuances of relocation to embracing cultural etiquette, managing transportation to celebrating milestones, you've gathered the tools needed to navigate the intricacies of life in Albania.

As you reflect on the pages turned and the chapters explored, remember that this guide is not a finite map but a compass—a tool that empowers you to continue your journey of discovery. Your Albanian adventure is an ongoing odyssey, and the concluding chapter is a reminder that every day in this vibrant nation is an opportunity for new experiences, deeper connections, and the creation of lasting memories.

Closing Thoughts: Your Personal Tapestry

As you conclude this guide, remember that your Albanian adventure is a personal tapestry—an intricate weaving of moments, encounters, and the unique story you're crafting. Albania, with its ancient history, warm hospitality, and diverse landscapes, has become more than a location; it's a part of your narrative, forever etched in the canvas of your life.

Every challenge overcome, every friend made, and every landscape explored adds depth to your personal tapestry. Whether you're sipping coffee in a quaint café, hiking along mountain trails, or celebrating local festivals, each moment contributes to the rich composition of your Albanian story.

So, as you continue your journey, embrace the unknown with curiosity, approach new experiences with an open heart, and let the tapestry of your Albanian adventure unfold organically. Whether you're creating connections in the vibrant streets of Tirana, basking in the sun on the Albanian Riviera, or simply enjoying the tranquility of a lakeside town, know that each moment is a stroke in the masterpiece of your unique journey.

In the symphony of life, where every experience is a note, Albania has offered you a melody that resonates with the beauty of discovery, the warmth of connections, and the enduring allure of a nation waiting to be explored. As you step forward into the next chapter of your Albanian adventure, may it be filled with continued wonder, growth, and the joy of crafting a tapestry that reflects the extraordinary richness of your journey in this captivating land.

Appendix

Checklist for Long-Term Success

Congratulations on embarking on your journey to relocate to Albania! To ensure a smooth transition and long-term success in your new adventure, consider the following checklist. This comprehensive guide will help you navigate the practicalities of living in Albania and make the most of your experience.

Before You Move:

- **Research and Learn About Albania:**
    - Understand the culture, customs, and basic Albanian phrases.
    - Explore online forums and expat communities to gain insights from those who have already moved.

- **Legal Requirements:**
    - Research visa and residence permit requirements.
    - Gather necessary documentation for the visa application process.

- **Healthcare:**
    - Check if your current health insurance covers international healthcare or consider purchasing international health insurance.
    - Research healthcare providers and facilities in Albania.

- **Finances:**
    - Notify your bank about your move and inquire about international banking services.
    - Set up online banking for easy management of

finances from abroad.

- ☐ **Accommodation:**
  - ◦ Research neighborhoods and housing options.
  - ◦ Consider temporary accommodation for your initial arrival.

- ☐ **Language Preparation:**
  - ◦ Start learning basic Albanian phrases.
  - ◦ Explore language learning apps and courses to enhance your language skills.

Upon Arrival:

- ☐ **Register with Authorities:**
  - ◦ Complete any required registration with local authorities.
  - ◦ Familiarize yourself with local laws and regulations.

- ☐ **Banking and Finances:**
  - ◦ Open a local bank account for easier transactions.
  - ◦ Set up online banking for convenient management of your finances.

- ☐ **Local SIM Card:**
  - ◦ Purchase a local SIM card for your phone.
  - ◦ Explore mobile service providers for the best plans that suit your needs.

- ☐ **Healthcare:**
  - ◦ Register with local healthcare services.
  - ◦ Familiarize yourself with the locations of hospitals and clinics in your area.

- ☐ **Utilities and Services:**

- Set up utilities such as electricity, water, and internet.
- Explore local service providers for cable, internet, and other essential services.

Integration and Lifestyle:

- **Cultural Immersion:**
  - Attend local events, festivals, and cultural activities.
  - Participate in language exchange programs to improve your language skills.

- **Social Connections:**
  - Join expat groups and social communities.
  - Attend local meetups and gatherings to meet new people.

- **Education and Schools:**
  - Enroll children in local schools or international schools if applicable.
  - Explore extracurricular activities and educational opportunities.

- **Employment Opportunities:**
  - If applicable, explore job opportunities and networking events.
  - Understand local employment laws and regulations.

- **Transportation:**
  - Familiarize yourself with local transportation options.
  - Obtain a local driver's license if necessary.

Ongoing Wellness:

- **Counseling and Support:**

- ○ Research counseling services and support groups.
- ○ Establish a network of friends and contacts for emotional support.

- ☐ **Explore Leisure Activities:**
  - ○ Discover outdoor activities, local attractions, and recreational opportunities.
  - ○ Join clubs or groups aligned with your hobbies and interests.

- ☐ **Maintain a Healthy Lifestyle:**
  - ○ Find local gyms, fitness classes, or outdoor exercise options.
  - ○ Explore local markets for fresh produce and ingredients.

- ☐ **Continued Learning:**
  - ○ Engage in ongoing language learning.
  - ○ Attend workshops or courses to enhance your skills and knowledge.

Emergency Preparedness:

- ☐ **Emergency Contacts:**
  - ○ Save local emergency numbers in your phone.
  - ○ Keep contact information for your country's embassy or consulate.

- ☐ **Health and Safety Precautions:**
  - ○ Stay informed about health and safety guidelines in your area.
  - ○ Familiarize yourself with evacuation procedures if living in an earthquake-prone region.

- ☐ **Important Documents:**

○ Keep copies of essential documents (passport, residence permit, insurance) in a secure location.
○ Share emergency contact information with a trusted friend or family member.

Regular Check-ins:

- ⌐ **Legal Updates:**
  ○ Stay updated on any changes to visa or residence permit requirements.
  ○ Renew documents as necessary.

- ⌐ **Cultural and Local News:**
  ○ Stay informed about local news and cultural events.
  ○ Subscribe to local newsletters or newspapers.

- ⌐ **Community Involvement:**
  ○ Continue engaging with local communities and events.
  ○ Explore opportunities for volunteering or contributing to local initiatives.

- ⌐ **Networking:**
  ○ Attend networking events to expand your professional and social circles.
  ○ Utilize online platforms to connect with other expats and locals.

Final Thoughts: Relocating to a new country is a transformative experience filled with challenges and rewards. This checklist is designed to guide you through the practical aspects of your move and help you build a successful and fulfilling life in Albania. As you navigate this exciting journey, remember to embrace the uniqueness of your experience, be open to new opportunities, and savor the moments that contribute to the richness of your life abroad. Here's to your long-term success and the adventures that await you in Albania!

Made in the USA
Coppell, TX
11 December 2024

42280452R00049